THE BASICS OF

FMEA

ROBIN E. MCDERMOTT
RAYMOND J. MIKULAK
MICHAEL R. BEAUREGARD

Productivity Press

New York

Productivity Press
444 Park Avenue South, 7th flr
New York, NY 10016
Telephone: 212-686-5900
Fax: 212-686-5411
Customer Service: 888-319-5852
E-mail: info@productivitypress.com

   Discounts are available for multiple copies through the Sales
Department (888-319-5852).

Printed in the United States of America

 06 07   13 12 11

ISBN 978-0-527-76320-6

CONTENTS

CONTENTS

Failure Mode and Effect Analysis (FMEA) techniques have been around for over 30 years. It is only recently, however, that FMEAs have gained widespread appeal outside the safety arena, thanks in large part to the U.S. automotive industry and its QS-9000 supplier requirements.

The QS-9000 standard requires suppliers to the automotive industry to conduct product/design and process FMEAs in an effort to eliminate failures before they happen.

Unlike many quality improvement tools, FMEAs do not require complicated statistics, yet they can yield significant savings for a company as well as reduce the potential costly liability of a process or product that does not perform as promised.

FMEAs do take time and people resources. Because they are team-based, several people will be involved in the process. The foundation of FMEAs is the input of the FMEA team members. Companies must be prepared to allow the team enough time to do a thorough job.

This booklet was designed to help FMEA teams reduce their learning curve and conduct effective and efficient FMEAs, starting with the first one done. The book's easy-to-use reference format makes it an invaluable resource for FMEA team meetings.

The FMEA process described here meets QS-9000 requirements, and is based on FMEA guidelines established by teams at Chrysler, Ford, and General Motors, working under the auspices of the Automotive Division of the American Society for Quality Control (ASQC) and the Automotive Industry Action Group (AIAG).

An FMEA is a systematic method of identifying and preventing product and process problems before they occur. FMEAs are focused on preventing defects, enhancing safety, and increasing customer satisfaction. Ideally, FMEAs are conducted in the product design or process development stages, although conducting an FMEA on existing products and processes may also yield huge benefits.

The History of FMEAs

The first formal FMEAs were conducted in the aerospace industry in the mid-1960s, specifically looking at safety issues. Before long, FMEAs became a key tool for improving safety, especially in the chemical process industries. The goal with safety FMEAs was, and remains today, to prevent safety accidents and incidents from occurring.

While engineers have always analyzed processes and products for potential failures, the FMEA process standardizes the approach and establishes a common language that can be used both within and between companies. It can also be used by nontechnical as well as technical employees of all levels.

The automotive industry adapted the FMEA technique, initially developed for safety improvement, for use as a quality improvement tool.

What Is the Purpose of an FMEA?

Preventing process and product problems before they occur is the purpose of Failure Mode and Effect Analysis, or FMEAs. Used in both the design and manufacturing process, they substantially reduce costs by identifying product and process improvements early in the development process when relatively easy and inexpensive changes can be made. The result is a more robust process and the reduction or elimination of the need for after-the-fact corrective action and late change crises.

Part of a Comprehensive Quality System

A formal FMEA process should be a part of a comprehensive quality system. While they can be effective used alone, a company will not get maximum benefit from FMEAs if systems are not in place to support and enhance them. For example, one element of a comprehensive quality system is effective use of data and information. Without reliable data on a product or process, the FMEA becomes a guessing game based on opinions rather than actual facts. The result may be that the FMEA team focuses on the wrong failure modes and misses significant opportunities to improve the failure modes that are the biggest problems. Another example that supports the need for a comprehensive quality system is documentation of procedures. This is especially critical with a process FMEA. In the absence of documented procedures, people working in the process could be introducing significant variation into the process by operating it slightly differently each time the process is run. In this case, the FMEA is aiming at a moving target because each time the process is run, it produces different results.

The key elements of a comprehensive quality system can be found in the Malcolm Baldrige National Quality Award, in the ISO 9000 and QS-9000 guidelines, as well as in various books and articles on the topic. Table 1 identifies 12 key elements and the role each plays in the FMEA process.

It is clear to see that without a comprehensive quality system, FMEAs will only be a fraction as effective as they should be.

FMEAs and Bottom Line Results

Effective use of FMEAs can have a positive impact on an organization's bottom line because of their preventive role. Here are three real examples.

Example 1
Ford required a manufacturer of automobile liquid-level floats to conduct both a design/product FMEA and a process FMEA. The manufacturer established three FMEA teams, each tasked with a different aspect of the process/product. Three team leaders were assigned and

Table 1. Twelve Key Elements of the FMEA Process

Quality System Element	Role in the FMEA Process
Leadership	Supports the FMEA process assuring the FMEA team has the necessary tools, resources, and time to work on the FMEA.
Strategic quality planning	Uses the results of FMEAs to assist in directing future improvement activities.
Process and business measures	Measures and monitors the results of FMEAs both in terms of product quality and bottom line results.
Effective use of data and information	Provides facts and data to confirm FMEA analysis and to measure the results of the FMEA process.
Process control (both the company's and the suppliers')	Assures a stable process and product at the start of an FMEA and statistically monitors improvements made through the FMEA process.
Human resources	Supports the FMEA team with appropriate training in quality improvement tools and techniques.
Training	Provides the basic skills necessary to work on an FMEA team, identify potential problems, and determine solutions.
A documented quality plan	Identifies FMEAs as part of the overall quality strategy of the company. Defines when and where FMEAs should be used and documents the FMEA process the FMEA teams should use.
Documented procedures	Assure that consistent operating methods are being used thus reducing unnecessary variation in the process and product.
Design control	Assures consistency in the design process.
Customer focus	Provides the team with information about what's important to the customer and information that can be incorporated in the FMEA process.
A customer feedback system	Provides the FMEA team with additional data to consider during the FMEA process.

were responsible for ensuring the team's efforts were coordinated.

The Results
- The combined efforts of the teams resulted in a decrease in defectives to 0.2 parts per million.

- The equipment uptime increased from 74% to 89%.

- Customer complaints dropped from an average of two per year to none.

- Productivity per labor hour increased by 22%.

Example 2
An aircraft engine manufacturer conducted an FMEA on its engine assembly operation. A cross-functional team was formed that included individuals from outside of the assembly department, although all were familiar with assembly to some extent.

The Results
- The team identified the biggest risk of failure and mistake-proofed the process to the point where there was no chance of it reoccurring.

- Internal failures dropped to one-third of what they had been, eliminating problems that had existed for years but were not high enough a priority to address until the FMEA.

- The manufacturer saved $6,000 per month on engine tear-downs.

Example 3

A small printed circuit board manufacturer with 35 employees formed an FMEA team. While the manager was a team member, his role was to keep notes, not to lead the team. After a brief FMEA training session, the team decided to collect data and information from other operators that were not on the team. With that information, they were able to complete the FMEA in four two-hour sessions.

The Results

- The highest priority items were associated with the wave-soldering operation.

- The team discovered that many of the failure modes were related to preventive maintenance of the soldering unit.

- After establishing and implementing a preventive maintenance program, the team decreased solder defects on the complex boards they manufactured from an average of 11 per board to an average of one per board. The team continues to work to further reduce the defects.

ISO 9000, QS-9000, and FMEAs

ISO 9000 certification means a company is capable of controlling the processes that determine the acceptability of its product or service. The standards were adopted by the International Organization for Standardization (ISO). Many organizations are required by their customers to be ISO 9000 or QS-9000 certified. Many other organizations seek certification without being required to do so by their customers. Regardless of why organizations initially engage in a certification effort, most find that the process is an excellent way to evaluate the existing quality system, identify the gaps, and develop and implement plans to narrow and eventually eliminate the gaps completely.

ISO 9000, the foundation of the QS-9000 system, identifies 20 elements of a quality system that are subject to a rigorous audit during the certification process. The elements include items such as management responsibility, design control, process control, inspection and testing, control of quality records, and corrective and preventive action, to name a few.

One of the ISO 9000 requirements is that the company engages in quality planning. In meeting the specified requirements for products, projects, or contracts, suppliers are to give consideration to, among other things, the following:

> *. . . ensuring the compatibility of the design, the production process, installation, servicing, inspection and test procedures, and the applicable documentation. . . .*

QS-9000 builds on ISO 9000 and gives an organization an even more detailed and specific framework for a comprehensive quality system. In many cases, QS-9000 defines specific actions required to fulfill the ISO requirement. The clauses related to FMEAs in the QS-9000 standard provide an excellent example of how the two standards work together. In the case of the ISO clause stated earlier, QS-9000 interprets and supplements the ISO 9000 requirement by stating that:

> *Suppliers shall establish and implement an advanced product quality planning process. Suppliers should convene internal cross-functional teams to prepare for production of new or changed products.*

The QS-9000 standard then suggests that team actions should include (among other things):

- *Development and review of FMEAs*

- *Establishment of actions to reduce the potential failure modes with high-risk priorities.*

The QS-9000 standard also clearly directs suppliers to use the FMEA process to improve the process to achieve defect prevention rather than defect detection.

While many organizations are undertaking FMEAs to meet the automotive industry's QS-9000 requirements, FMEAs are valuable to any type of business, manufacturing or service, in the design, development, and on-going improvement of their products and processes.

For further information on these issues, see these publications by the Automotive Industry Action Group (AIAG):

Potential Failure Mode and Effect Analysis, 2nd ed., February 1995.

Quality System Requirements: QS-9000, 2nd ed., February 1995.

The FMEA Process

The objective of an FMEA is to look for all of the ways a process or product can fail. A product failure occurs when the product does not function as it should or when it malfunctions in some way. Even the simplest products have many opportunities for failure. For example, a drip coffeemaker—a relatively simple household appliance—could have several things fail that would render the coffeemaker inoperable. Here are some possible ways the coffeemaker can fail:

- Heating element does not heat water to sufficient temperature to brew coffee.

- Pump does not pump water into the filter basket.

- Coffeemaker does not turn on automatically by the clock.

- Clock stops working or runs too fast or too slow.

- Calcium deposits from impure water clog up the brewing process.

- Not enough or too much coffee is used.

- There is a short in the electrical cord.

Failures are not limited to problems with the product. Because failures also can occur when the user makes a mistake, those types of failures should be included in the FMEA. Anything that can be done to assure the product works correctly, regardless of how the user operates it, will move the product closer to 100% total customer satisfaction.

Ways in which a product or process can fail are called failure modes. Each failure mode has a potential effect, and some effects are more likely to occur than others. In addition, each potential effect has a relative risk associated with it. The FMEA process is a way to identify the failures, effects, and risks within a process or product, and then eliminate or reduce them.

Evaluating the Risk of Failure

The relative risk of a failure and its effects is determined by three factors:

- **Severity**—the consequence of the failure should it occur.

- **Occurrence**—the probability or frequency of the failure occurring.

- **Detection**—the probability of the failure being detected before the impact of the effect is realized.

Assessing the Risk Priority Number

Using data and knowledge of the process or product, each potential failure mode and effect is rated in each of these three factors on a scale ranging from 1 to 10, low to high.

By multiplying the rating for the three factors (severity × occurrence × detection), a **risk priority number** or **RPN** will be determined for each potential failure mode and effect.

The risk priority number (which will range from 1 to 1,000 for each failure mode) is used to rank the need for corrective actions to eliminate or reduce the potential failure modes. Those failure modes with the highest RPNs should be attended to first, although special attention should be given when the severity rating is high (9 or 10) regardless of the RPN.

Once corrective action has been taken, a new RPN is determined by reevaluating the Severity, Occurrence, and Detection ratings. This new RPN is called the **Resulting RPN**. Improvement and corrective action must continue until the resulting RPN is at an acceptable level for all potential failure modes.

Although one person typically is responsible for coordinating the FMEA process, all FMEAs are team based. The purpose for an FMEA team is to bring a variety of perspectives and experiences to the project.

Because each FMEA is unique in dealing with different aspects of the product or process, FMEA teams are formed when needed and disbanded once the FMEA is complete. In fact, it would be inappropriate to establish a permanent FMEA team because the composition of the team is dictated by the specific task or objective. In cases where several FMEAs are needed to cover one process or product, it is good practice to have some overlap of membership between the teams, but there also should be some members who serve on only one or two of the teams to assure a fresh perspective of the potential problems and solutions.

FMEA Team Size

The best size for the team is usually four to six people, but the minimum number of people will be dictated by the number of areas that are affected by the FMEA. Each area (for example, manufacturing, engineering, maintenance, materials, and technical service) should be represented on the team. The customer of the process, whether internal or external to the organization, can add another unique perspective as well and should be considered for team membership.

FMEA Team Membership

It is helpful also to have people on the team who have different levels of familiarity with the product or process. Those who are most familiar with it will have valuable insights, but may overlook some of the most obvious potential problems. Those who are less familiar with the process or product will bring unbiased, objective ideas into the FMEA process. Be aware that those with an emotional investment in the process or product may be overly sensitive during the critiquing process and may become defensive. Deciding whether to include them on the team must involve weighing the disadvantages against the advantages that their experience and knowledge will bring to the process.

FMEA Team Leader

An FMEA team leader should be appointed by management or selected by the team as soon as it is assembled. The team leader is responsible for coordinating the FMEA process, including:

- Setting up and facilitating meetings.

- Ensuring the team has the necessary resources available.

- Making sure the team is progressing toward the completion of the FMEA.

The team leader should not dominate the team and does not normally have the final word on team decisions. The team leader's role is more like that of a facilitator than a decision-maker.

Arrangements should be made for someone to be responsible for taking meeting minutes and maintaining the FMEA records. The scribe's role is often rotated among all team members, except the team leader. This spreads the burden of recording the meeting equally among all participants.

The Role of the Process Expert

A point that is often debated with FMEAs is what role the process expert(s) plays on the FMEA team. A person with expertise in the process (for example, the design engineer in a design FMEA or the process engineer in a process FMEA) can bring tremendous insight to the team and can help speed the process. In many ways he or she can be a real asset to the team. On the other hand, a process expert can also slow the FMEA process.

An FMEA is a critical look at a product or process. People on the FMEA team who have a stake in the product or process being examined cannot allow their egos to get in the way of the FMEA. This is especially difficult for the process expert. Most likely he or she has a huge investment in the process or product, both in terms of time and personal integrity. The purpose of an FMEA, in essence, is to find flaws in that person's work. This can be a difficult process for an individual to go through and may result in several different types of reactions including defensiveness, anger, and decreased self-esteem, all of which are counterproductive for both the team and the process expert.

Training the FMEA Team

While it is helpful for FMEA team members to have some understanding of the FMEA process before starting the project (such as reading through this book and having it handy as a reference), extensive training is not necessary if team members have previous experience working on problem-solving teams. A team leader or facilitator who is well versed in the FMEA process can easily guide the team through the process as they are actually performing the FMEA. This means that there is not a need for extensive classroom training. Instead, the FMEA team can immediately be productive working on a real FMEA project and at the same time benefit from the most powerful form of training—experience.

It is important, however, that FMEA team members know the basics of working on a team because they will be using those skills as FMEA team members. Knowledge of consensus-building techniques, team project documentation, and idea-generating techniques such as brainstorming are all necessary for FMEA team members. In addition, team members should be comfortable using continuous improvement problem-solving tools such as flowcharting, data analysis, and graphing techniques.

FMEA Boundaries of Freedom

It is important that the FMEA team has clearly defined boundaries within which they are free to conduct the FMEA and suggest and implement improvements. For example:

- Is the team responsible only for conducting the analysis, are they to make recommendations for improvements, and/or are they to implement the improvements?

- What is their spending budget?

- What other resources do they have at their disposal?

- Does the team face a deadline or other time constraints?

- What process must they follow if they need to expand beyond the defined boundaries?

- What and how should they communicate the FMEA process and results to others in the organization?

Management is responsible for defining the boundaries of freedom. Some of the boundaries can be standing guidelines for all FMEA teams. For example, a standard procedure can be established to define the process that teams must follow if they need to go beyond the normal boundaries, and this procedure can apply to all FMEA teams. The same holds true for the process that the team should use to communicate the FMEA results to others in the organization. Other boundaries will need to be set for each FMEA and will depend on the type of FMEA (design/product or process), the scope of the FMEA, and the people on the FMEA team.

While management is responsible for defining the boundaries of freedom, the FMEA team members have equal responsibility in making sure these boundaries are defined before the project gets underway. If the team members do not know what the boundaries are or if they are unclear about any of the boundaries, they should get clarification before proceeding with the FMEA. This will help the team avoid problems and conflicts later in the process.

FMEA Scope

The scope of the FMEA must be well defined. This definition usually comes from the leader of the function responsible for the FMEA. If the FMEA is focused on the design of a product, the head of the design function should clearly define the scope of the project. For a process FMEA, the leader of the manufacturing or manufacturing–engineering function would most likely define the scope.

A specific and clear definition of the process or product to be studied should be written and understood by everyone on the team. Team members should have an opportunity to clarify their understanding of the scope, if necessary, and those clarifications should be documented. This will help prevent the team from focusing on the wrong aspect of the product or process during the FMEA.

For example, if your team is working on a product FMEA on a new drip coffeemaker that your company has just developed, your definition of the product to be studied might be:

> *Our team will conduct an FMEA on the new RS-100 coffeemaker and the glass carafe for that coffeemaker. The FMEA will not include any parts of this coffeemaker that are common to other coffeemakers in our product line such as the electronic clock, the electrical cord and wiring into the coffeemaker, and the gold cone coffee filter.*

A specific and clear definition is even more important with process FMEAs because they can encompass so many different aspects of the process manufacturing chain from the raw materials to components, to the actual manufacturing and assembly, to the shipping, and everything in between. While each part of the chain plays an important role in the quality of a product, it may help to use a narrow definition of the process to assure that the FMEA project is completed in a timely manner.

Because large processes may be difficult to work on

in their entirety, break them into subprocesses when possible and attend to them one at a time, or have several teams working at the same time on different subprocesses.

FMEA Start-Up Worksheet

The FMEA Start-Up Worksheet, shown in Figure 1, can help the members of a team make sure they have a clear understanding of their boundaries of freedom and team member roles and responsibilities before the project gets underway.

Figure 1. FMEA Team Start-Up Worksheet

FMEA Number: _____   Date Started: _____

Date Completed: _____

Team Members: _____   _____   _____

_____   _____   _____

_____   _____   _____

Team Leader: _____

1. Are all affected areas represented?

    YES   NO   Action: _____

2. Are different levels and types of knowledge represented on the team?

    YES   NO   Action: _____

3. Is the customer involved?

    YES   NO   Action: _____

4. Who will take minutes and maintain records? _____

FMEA Team Boundaries of Freedom

5. What aspects of the FMEA is the team responsible for?

    FMEA Analysis   Recommendations for Improvement   Implementation of Improvements

6. What is the budget for the FMEA? _____

7. Does the project have a deadline? _____

8. Do team members have specific time constraints? _____

9. What is the procedure if the team needs to expand beyond these boundaries?

_____

10. How should the FMEA be communicated to others? _____

11. What is the scope of the FMEA? (Be specific and include a clear definition of the process on product to be studied.)

_____

_____

_____

The principles and steps behind all FMEAs, whether they are focused on the product or the process, are the same even though the objectives may differ.

Product/Design

- The objective for a product or design FMEA is to uncover problems with the product that will result in safety hazards, product malfunctions, or a shortened product life. As consumers, we are all too familiar with examples of these types of problems such as an air bag in a car that may not work properly or a paint job that cracks and dulls within the first three or four years that you own the car.

- Product FMEAs can be conducted at each phase in the design process (preliminary design, prototype, or final design) or they can be used on products that are already in production. The key question asked in design FMEAs is, ''How can the product fail?''

Process

- Process FMEAs uncover process problems related to the manufacture of the product. For example, a piece of automated assembly equipment may misfeed parts resulting in products not being assembled correctly. Or, in a chemical manufacturing process, temperature and mixing time could be sources of potential failures resulting in unusable product.

- It is helpful when conducting a process FMEA to think in terms of the five elements of a process: people, materials, equipment, methods, and environment. With these five elements in mind, ask, "How can process failure affect the product, processing efficiency, or safety?"

Both types of FMEAs use severity, occurrence, and detection ratings, although the definitions of the rating scale for each may be different. Many organizations have different customized rating scales for their product FMEAs and process FMEAs. The rating scales presented in this book are suggestions and can be used as starting points to customize a rating scale for your organization.

All product/design and process FMEAs follow these 10 steps:

- Step 1: Review the process.

- Step 2: Brainstorm potential failure modes.

- Step 3: List potential effects of each failure mode.

- Step 4: Assign a severity rating for each effect.

- Step 5: Assign an occurrence rating for each failure mode.

- Step 6: Assign a detection rating for each failure mode and/or effect.

- Step 7: Calculate the risk priority number for each effect.

- Step 8: Prioritize the failure modes for action.

- Step 9: Take action to eliminate or reduce the high-risk failure modes.

- Step 10: Calculate the resulting RPN as the failure modes are reduced or eliminated.

These steps are explained in detail following the FMEA worksheet section, and are illustrated in a case study.

The FMEA Worksheet

The FMEA process should be documented using the FMEA worksheet (see Figure 2). This form captures all of the important information about the FMEA and serves as an excellent communication tool. Some organizations have their own format for the FMEA worksheet. Others will adapt this form to meet their needs.

The worksheet is easiest to work with when enlarged to an 11″ × 17″ size or when put on an overhead slide for use during team meetings.

A numbering system to track and access FMEA projects is helpful. The numbering system should enable cross-referencing to similar FMEAs as well as other improvement activities dealing with the same product or process.

Copies of all FMEAs should be kept in a central location so they are easily accessible during audits or internal process and product reviews.

Step 1: Review the Process

To ensure that everyone on the FMEA team has the same understanding of the process that is being worked on, the team should review a blueprint (or engineering drawing) of the product if they are conducting a product FMEA, or a detailed flowchart of the operation if they are conducting a process FMEA.

If a blueprint or flowchart is not available, the team will need to create one prior to starting the FMEA pro-

Figure 2. Potential Failure Mode and Effect Analysis

Process/Product: _____

FMEA Team: _____

Team Leader: _____

FMEA Number: _____

FMEA Date: (Original) _____

(Revised) _____

Page: ___ of ___

Item and Function	Potential Failure Mode	Potential Effect(s) of Failure	Severity	Potential Cause(s) of Failure	Occurrence	Current Controls	Detection	RPN	Recommended Action	Responsibility and Target Completion Date	Action Taken	Severity	Occurrence	Detection	RPN

FMEA Process — Action Results

Total Risk Priority Number

Resulting Risk Priority Number

cess. (Information on creating a flowchart can be found in Appendix 1.)

With the blueprint or flowchart in hand, the team members should familiarize themselves with the product or process. For a product FMEA, they should physically see the product or a prototype of the product. For a process FMEA, the team should physically walk through the process exactly as the process flows.

It is helpful to have an ''expert'' on the product or process available to answer any questions the team might have.

Step 2: Brainstorm Potential Failure Modes

Once everyone on the team has an understanding of the process (or product), team members can begin thinking about potential failure modes that could affect the manufacturing process or the product quality. A brainstorming session will get all of those ideas out on the table. Team members should come to the brainstorming meeting with a list of their ideas. In addition to the ideas members bring to the meeting, others will be generated as a result of the synergy of the group process.

Because of the complexity of most manufactured products and manufacturing processes, it is best to conduct a series of brainstorming sessions, each focused on a different element (for example; people, methods, equipment, materials, and the environment) of the product or process. Focusing on the elements one at a time will result in a more thorough list of potential failure modes.

It is not unusual to generate dozens of ideas from the brainstorming process. In fact, that's the objective!

Once the brainstorming is complete, the ideas should be organized by grouping them into like categories. Your team must decide the best categories for grouping, as there are many different ways to form groups with failure modes. You can group them by the type of failure (e.g., electrical, mechanical, user-created), where on the product or process the failure occurred, or the seriousness (at least the team's best guess at this point) of the failure. Grouping the failures will make the FMEA process easier to work through. Without the grouping step, the team may invest a lot of energy jumping from one aspect of the product to a completely different aspect of the product and then back again. An easy way to work through the grouping process is to put all of the failure modes onto self-stick notes and post them on a wall so they are easy to see and move around as they are being grouped.

The grouping also gives the team a chance to consider whether some failure modes should be combined, because they are the same or very similar to each other. When the failure modes have been grouped and combined, if appropriate, they should be transferred onto the FMEA sheet. The example in Figure 3 shows how each part of the process or piece of the product and its function are listed followed by the potential failure modes associated with that item.

Figure 3. Failure Mode and Effect Analysis Worksheet

Process/Product: Fire Extinguisher

FMEA Team: Fire Extinguisher FMEA Team

Team Leader: Kevin M

Item and Function	Potential Failure Mode	Potential Effect(s) of Failure	Severity	Potential Cause(s) of Failure	Occurrence	Current Controls	Detection	RPN	Recommended Action	Responsibility and Target Completion Date	Action Taken	Severity	Occurrence	Detection	RPN
Hose	Cracks														
	Pinholes														
	Blockages														
Canister	Paint coverage uneven														
	Canister dented														
	Label not properly glued														
Charge Gauge	Inaccurate reading														
	Broken crystal														
Valve Mechanism	Safety pin missing														
	Handle freezes														

Step 3: List Potential Effects
of Each Failure Mode

With the failure modes listed on the FMEA Data Collection Form, the FMEA team reviews each failure mode and identifies the potential effects of the failure should it occur. For some of the failure modes, there may be only one effect while there may be several effects for other failure modes.

This step must be thorough, because this information will feed into the assignment of risk ratings for each of the failures. It is helpful to think of this step as an if-then process: *If* the failure occurs, *then* what are the consequences.

Steps 4, 5, and 6: Assigning
Severity, Occurrence, and
Detection Ratings

Each of these three ratings are based on a 10-point scale, with 1 being the lowest rating and 10 being the highest.

It is important to establish clear and concise descriptions for the points on each of the scales, so that all team members have the same understanding of the ratings. The scales should be established before the team begins the rating process. The more descriptive the team is when defining the rating scale, the easier it should be to reach consensus during the rating process.

A generic rating system for each of the scales is provided in Tables 2, 3 and 4. This system should be customized by the team for their specific FMEA project or, even better, customized by the organization for all FMEAs.

Even if the rating system is clear and concise, there still may be disagreement about the rating for a particular item. In these cases, the techniques described in Appendix 3, may help the group reach consensus.

Step 4: Assign a Severity Rating for Each Effect

The severity rating is an estimation of how serious the effects would be if a given failure did occur. In some cases it is clear, because of past experience, how serious the problem would be. In other cases, it is necessary to estimate the severity based on the knowledge and expertise of the team members.

Because each failure may have several different effects, and each effect can have a different level of severity, it is the effect, not the failure, that is rated. Therefore, each effect should be given its own severity rating, even if there are several effects for a single failure mode.

Table 2. Severity Rating Scale*

Rating	Description	Definition
10	Dangerously high	Failure could injure the customer or an employee.
9	Extremely high	Failure would create noncompliance with federal regulations.
8	Very high	Failure renders the unit inoperable or unfit for use.
7	High	Failure causes a high degree of customer dissatisfaction.
6	Moderate	Failure results in a subsystem or partial malfunction of the product.
5	Low	Failure creates enough of a performance loss to cause the customer to complain.
4	Very Low	Failure can be overcome with modifications to the customer's process or product, but there is minor performance loss.
3	Minor	Failure would create a minor nuisance to the customer, but the customer can overcome it in the process or product without performance loss.
2	Very Minor	Failure may not be readily apparent to the customer, but would have minor effects on the customer's process or product.
1	None	Failure would not be noticeable to the customer and would not affect the customer's process or product.

*Should be modified to fit the specific product or process.

Step 5: Assign an Occurrence Rating for Each Failure Mode

The best method for determining the occurrence rating is to use actual data from the process. This may be in the form of failure logs or even process capability data. When actual failure data are not available, the team must estimate how often a failure mode may occur. The team can make a better estimate of how likely a failure mode is to occur and at what frequency by knowing the potential cause of failure. Once the potential causes have been identified for all of the failure modes, an occurrence rating can be assigned even without failure data.

Step 6: Assign a Detection Rating for Each Failure Mode and/or Effect

The detection rating looks at how likely we are to detect a failure or the effect of a failure. We start this step by identifying current controls that may detect a failure or effect of a failure. If there are no current controls, the likelihood of detection will be low, and the item would receive a high rating, such as a 9 or 10. The current controls should be listed first for all of the failure modes, or the effects of the failures and then the detection ratings assigned.

Table 3. Occurrence Rating Scale*

Rating	Description	Potential Failure Rate
10	Very High: Failure is almost inevitable	More than one occurrence per day or a probability of more than three occurrences in 10 events ($C_{pk} < 0.33$).
9		One occurrence every three to four days or a probability of three occurrences in 10 events ($C_{pk} \approx 0.33$).
8	High: Repeated failures	One occurrence per week or a probability of 5 occurrences in 100 events ($C_{pk} \approx 0.67$).
7		One occurrence every month or one occurrence in 100 events ($C_{pk} \approx 0.83$).
6	Moderate: Occasional failures	One occurrence every three months or three occurrences in 1,000 events ($C_{pk} \approx 1.00$).
5		One occurrence every six months to one year or one occurrence in 10,000 events ($C_{pk} \approx 1.17$)
4		One occurrence per year or six occurrences in 100,000 events ($C_{pk} \approx 1.33$).
3	Low: Relatively few failures	One occurrence every one to three years or six occurrences in ten million events ($C_{pk} \approx 1.67$).
2		One occurrence every three to five years or 2 occurrences in one billion events ($C_{pk} \approx 2.00$).
1	Remote: Failure is unlikely.	One occurrence in greater than five years or less than two occurrences in one billion events ($C_{pk} > 2.00$).

*Should be modified to fit the specific product or process.

Table 4. Detection Rating Scale*

Rating	Description	Definition
10	Absolute Uncertainty	The product is not inspected or the defect caused by failure is not detectable.
9	Very Remote	Product is sampled, inspected, and released based on Acceptable Quality Level (AQL) sampling plans.
8	Remote	Product is accepted based on no defectives in a sample.
7	Very Low	Product is 100% manually inspected in the process.
6	Low	Product is 100% manually inspected using go/no-go or other mistake-proofing gauges.
5	Moderate	Some Statistical Process Control (SPC) is used in process and product is final inspected off-line.
4	Moderately High	SPC is used and there is immediate reaction to out-of-control conditions.
3	High	An effective SPC program is in place with process capabilities (C_{pk}) greater than 1.33.
2	Very High	All product is 100% automatically inspected.
1	Almost Certain	The defect is obvious or there is 100% automatic inspection with regular calibration and preventive maintenance of the inspection equipment.

*Should be modified to fit the specific product or process.

Step 7: Calculate the Risk Priority Number for Each Failure Mode

The risk priority number (RPN) is simply calculated by multiplying the severity rating times the occurrence rating times the detection rating for all of the items.

$$\text{Risk Priority Number} = \text{Severity} \times \text{Occurrence} \times \text{Detection}$$

The total risk priority number should be calculated by adding all of the risk priority numbers. This number alone is meaningless, because each FMEA has a different number of failure modes and effects. However, it will serve as a gauge to compare the revised total RPN against the original RPN once the recommended actions have been instituted.

Step 8: Prioritize the Failure Modes for Action

The failure modes can now be prioritized by ranking them in order from the highest risk priority number to the smallest. A Pareto diagram is helpful to visualize the differences between the various ratings (see Figure 4).

The team must now decide which items to work on. Usually it helps to set a cut-off RPN, where any failure modes with an RPN above that point are attended to. Those below the cut-off are left alone for the time being. For example, an organization may decide that any RPN

Figure 4. Pareto Diagram of Ratings

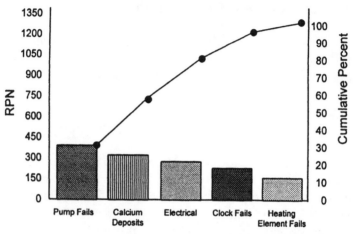

Note: The RPN for an individual failure mode will never exceed 1000. The RPN scale on this graph exceeds 1000 because the cumulative percent is calculated from the total RPN. The 100 percent point on the cumulative percent scale corresponds to the total RPN for all failure modes on the RPN scale.

above 200 creates an unacceptable risk. This decision sets the cut-off RPN at 200.

Step 9: Take Action to Eliminate or Reduce the High-Risk Failure Modes

Using an organized problem-solving process, identify and implement actions to eliminate or reduce the high-risk failure modes.

Ideally, the failure modes should be eliminated completely. For example, gasoline companies, car manufacturers, and pump manufacturers worked together during the phaseout of leaded fuel to eliminate the potential failure mode of putting leaded fuel into a car that runs on unleaded fuel. This was accomplished by making the gas tank opening too small for the leaded gas nozzle.

When a failure mode has been eliminated completely, the new risk priority number becomes zero because the occurrence rating becomes zero.

While elimination of failure modes altogether is ideal, it may not be achievable in all cases. When this happens, it helps to refer back to the severity, occurrence, and detection ratings that the team assigned to each item. Think of ways to reduce the ratings on one, two, or all three of the scales.

Often, the easiest approach to make a process or product improvement is to increase the detectability of the failure, thus lowering the detection rating. For example, a coffeemaker might have a tone that sounds every 10 minutes to remind you that it is turned on and that you need to turn it off before you leave the house, or a computer manufacturer may include a piece of software that notifies the user that there is low disk space.

However, these are Band-Aid approaches which often are costly and do not actually improve the quality of the product. Increasing failure detectability will simply make it easier to detect failures once they occur.

Reducing the severity is important, especially in situations that can lead to injuries. For example, a company that manufactures weed wackers might limit the speed of the machine reducing the severity of a potential personal injury. However, the richest opportunity for improvement lies in reducting of the likelihood of occurrence of the failure. After all, if it is highly unlikely that a failure will occur, there is less need for detection measures.

Table 5 identifies specific actions that can be taken to reduce the severity, occurrence, and detection ratings.

Step 10: Calculate the Resulting RPN as the Failure Modes Are Reduced

Once action has been taken to improve the product or process, new ratings for severity, occurrence, and detection should be determined, and a resulting RPN calculated.

For the failure modes where action was taken, there should be a significant reduction in the RPN. If not, that means the action did not reduce the severity, likelihood of occurrence, or detectability.

The resulting RPNs can be organized on a Pareto diagram and compared with the original RPNs. In addition, the total RPNs of the before-and-after product or process can be compared and contrasted. You should expect at least a 50% or greater reduction in the total RPN after an FMEA.

There is no target RPN for FMEAs. It is up to the

Table 5. Specific Actions to Reduce Ratings

Severity	Occurrence	Detection
• Personal Protective Equipment (e.g., hard hats or bump caps, side shields on safety glasses, full face protection, cut-proof gloves, long gloves). • Safety stops/emergency shut-offs. • Use different materials such as safety glass that will not cause as severe an injury should it fail.	• Increasing the C_{pk} through design of experiments and/or equipment modifications. • Focus on continuous improvement/problem solving teams. • Engaging mechanism that must be activated for the product or process to work (e.g., some lawn mowers have handles that must be squeezed in order for them to operate).	• Statistical process control (to monitor the process and identify when the process is going out of control). • Ensure the measuring devices are accurate and regularly calibrated. • Institute preventive maintenance to detect problems before they occur. • Use coding such as colors and shapes to alert the user or worker that something is either right or wrong.

FMEA team and the company to decide on how far the team should go with improvements.

There will always be the potential for failure modes to occur. The question the company must ask is how much relative risk the team is willing to take. That answer will depend on the industry and the seriousness of failure. For example, in the nuclear industry, there is little margin for error; they cannot risk a disaster occurring. In other industries, it may be acceptable to take higher risks. If the team is satisfied with the resulting RPN, it should present the FMEA results to management, who will determine if additional work should be done to further reduce the RPNs.

This example of a design/product FMEA involves a manufacturer of fire extinguishers. The company developed a new extinguisher for home use. It wanted to make sure the extinguisher would be effective and would not cause any problems when used. The consequences of a faulty extinguisher could be life-threatening.

A team of five employees was formed to work through the FMEA process. The team included a design engineer who helped develop the extinguisher, the second-shift manufacturing supervisor, the first-shift quality technician, the purchasing manager, and the sales and marketing manager. The design engineer was appointed the team leader, and the members decided to name their team ''The Fire Extinguisher FMEA Team.''

The team boundaries were to complete the FMEA, including making improvements. The team was given a $5,000 budget, and could request help from within the company to take the actions outside team members' expertise. The deadline for the project was a completion date of April 15, at which time another team would be formed to conduct a process FMEA.

Case Study Step 1: Review the Process

All team members were given a blueprint of the fire extinguisher to review. The design engineer brought a prototype extinguisher to the first meeting, and demonstrated how it worked. He also handed out a product specification sheet. Everyone on the team was given an opportunity to operate the extinguisher, and several good questions were asked and answered regarding the similarities and differences between the new extinguisher and existing models. For example, the product manager demonstrated how the extinguisher worked highlighting the differences in operation between the new and the existing models. One participant asked if this extinguisher would work the same for left- and right-handed people as do the existing models. Another wanted to know the benefits of the rounder shape of the canister.

The team also used the FMEA Team Start-Up Worksheet (see Figure 5) as a checklist to make sure they understood their boundaries of freedom and the scope of the project.

Case Study Step 2: Brainstorm Potential Failure Modes

As suggested in the guidelines, rather than dealing with the entire product at once, the team broke it into manageable chunks. The most logical breakdown was into the key components of the extinguisher: the hose, the canister, the charge gauge, and the valve mechanism. The chemical agent in the extinguisher was excluded because another team had included it in an FMEA about six months earlier.

The team then brainstormed all of the potential fail-

Figure 5. FMEA Team Start-Up Worksheet

FMEA Number:	*019*	Date Started:	*March 5*

Date Completed.

Team Members:	*Kevin M.*	*Shane T.*	*K.C. McG.*
	Chase L.	*Tyler J.*	

Team Leader. *Kevin M.*

1. Are all affected areas represented?

   (YES)   NO   Action.

2. Are different levels and types of knowledge represented on the team?

   (YES)   NO   Action

3. Is the customer involved?

   YES   (NO)   Action   *Sales and marketing will represent the customer.*

4. Who will take minutes and maintain records?   *Shane T.*

FMEA Team Boundaries of Freedom

5. What aspects of the FMEA is the team responsible for?

   (FMEA Analysis)   (Recommendations for Improvement)   (Implementation of Improvements)

6. What is the budget for the FMEA?   *$5,000.00*

7. Does the project have a deadline?   *April 15*

8. Do team members have specific time constraints?   *Hold a review with the FMEA Steering Committee.*

9. What is the procedure if the team needs to expand beyond these boundaries?
   Review with department managers by 3/15.

10. How should the FMEA be communicated to others?   *Report after completion.*

11. What is the scope of the FMEA? (Be specific and include a clear definition of the process on product to be studied.)
    This FMEA is focused on the new X-1050 model fire extinguisher. It is a product/design

    FMEA, and should not overlap with the process FMEA that will be conducted in May.

ures for each of those components. For example, with the hose, potential failures were cracks, holes, and blockages. With the canister, one potential failure was that the canister could be dented, and another was that the label might not be properly glued. They listed the potential failures on the FMEA Analysis worksheet, grouped by component (see Figure 3, p. 32).

Case Study Step 3: List Potential Effects of Each Failure Mode

Each failure mode was discussed, and the team agreed on potential effects for each of the failure modes. While there was some disagreement about the likelihood that a certain effect would occur, the team agreed to include all possible effects. Members reasoned that if it was highly unlikely that the failure and effect would occur, then the item would probably get a low RPN anyway.

The team listed each potential effect next to the failure. If members felt that several different effects were possible, and anticipated that each might have a different rating in at least one of the three rating categories, they listed them in a separate row.

Case Study Step 4: Assign a Severity Rating for Each Effect

Because a failure can have several different effects, and each effect can have a different level of severity associated with it, the team gave each effect its own severity rating. In most cases, members agreed on the severity rating, although in a couple of instances they had heated discussions before reaching consensus. In one of those cases, the team could not agree on a rating and had to hold a vote. Each member voted the score they felt the item should get, and the final rating was an average of all of the votes.

Case Study Step 5: Assign an Occurrence Rating for Each Failure Mode

The team began this step by collecting data on failures with similar fire extinguishers. For the failure modes where no data existed, the team identified the potential causes of failure associated with each failure mode. Not only did this information help members determine the likelihood of the failure occurring, but it also helped them target their improvement efforts once they had decided on the items they needed to improve.

Case Study Step 6: Assign a Detection Rating for Each Failure Mode and/or Effect

The Fire Extinguisher FMEA Team listed all controls currently in place for each of the potential causes of failure or the effect of the failure, and then assigned a detection rating for each item.

Case Study Step 7: Calculate the Risk Priority Number for Each Failure Mode

The RPN was calculated for each potential failure mode by multiplying the severity times the occurrence times the detection rating. The team noted that there were significant differences among the ratings, which made it easy to distinguish between the items that required action and those that could be left as is. The highest score was 600 points, and the lowest was 40 points.

Case Study Step 8: Prioritize the Failure Modes for Action

One of the team members created a Pareto diagram of the failure modes so that it would be easy to distinguish visually between the items. The team decided it would work on any item that had an RPN of 200 or higher. Two-hundred was set as the cut-off point because it encompassed over half of all of the potential failure modes. The team rationalized that an improvement in more than half of the failure modes would be a significant step in the right direction.

With the criteria of an RPN of 200 or higher, there were eight items they would need to attend to.

Case Study Step 9: Take Action to Eliminate or Reduce the High-Risk Failure Modes

Each of the high-risk failure modes was discussed, and the team determined what action would be taken to reduce the risk, assigning responsibility and a target completion date for each failure mode. The target was to have all of the action complete within six weeks, to give the team time to reevaluate the severity, occurrence, and detection of each item and determine what other work needed to be done before the product introduction date.

Case Study Step 10: Calculate the Resulting RPN as the Failure Modes are Reduced or Eliminated

After completing the corrective action, the team met, and all members responsible for an action item gave a report. All commitments were met, and the team was able to conduct its reevaluation FMEA at that same meeting.

There were only a couple of cases where severity reduced, but this didn't surprise the team because members knew that severity is the most difficult rating to impact. In some cases they were able to reduce the occurrence rating to zero by using mistake-proofing techniques. In others, they improved the detection ratings.

The team's efforts resulted in more than a 60 percent reduction in the resulting RPN from the original FMEA total RPN for all items. The eight areas addressed were at or below the target of 200 points. Pleased with the results, team members prepared their final report for management (see Figure 6).

Figure 6. Failure Mode and Effect Analysis Worksheet

Process/Product: Fire Extinguisher

FMEA Team: Fire Extinguisher FMEA Team

Team Leader: Kevin M.

Item and Function	Potential Failure Mode	Potential Effect(s) of Failure	Severity	Potential Cause(s) of Failure	Occurrence	Current Controls	Detection	RPN	Recommended Action	Responsibility and Target Completion Date	Action Taken	Severity	Occurrence	Detection	RPN
						FMEA Process					**Action Results**				
Hose	Cracks	Misfiring	010	Exposure to excessive heat or cold during shipping	005	- Insulated packaging materials - Climatic controlled shipping to retailers	006	300	Use hose that is not temperature-sensitive	Kevin 4/1	Changed to a nontemperature sensitive hose	010	002	006	120
	Pinholes	Low discharge pressure	008	Damage to the hose during manufacturing	008	- No sharp objects used in the hose operations	004	256	Put a protective Kevlar coating on the hose	K.C. 4/5	Purchasing puncture resistant cover for hose	008	005	004	160
	Blockages	No discharge	010	Foreign object in the hose	006	- Incoming inspection and hose pressure/air passage test	003	180	None			010	006	003	180
Canister	Paint coverage uneven	Bare metal spots rust causing weakened metal and possible explosion	010	Paint line runs low on paint	006	Automated inventory management system	002	120	None			010	006	002	120
			010	Spray painter nozzle gets partiall blocked	009	Regular nozzle cleaning procedure	004	360	Do not allow paint to dry on nozzles between use. Keep the nozzle in turpentine when not in use.	Tyler 3/15	Instituted new manufacturing procedures	010	003	004	120

Item	Potential Failure Mode / Effects	Potential Cause	Occ	Current Controls	Det	RPN	Recommended Action	Responsibility	Action Taken	Sev	Occ	Det	RPN
Canister dented	Metal weakened, possible explosion	Dropping the canister during manufacturing	010	Packing on floors where the canister is picked up	010	600	Design a canister grabbing device for operator to use	Kevin 4/1	Designed a device to handle the canisters. Now on order	010	003	006	180
Label not properly glued	Canister slips out of hands in use	Change in the type of glue	008	Glue standards established	003	48	None			008	003	002	48
	Operating instructions not readable	Excessive humidity	007	Climate control in the manufacturing plant	005	140	None			007	005	004	140
Charge Gauge	Inaccurate reading: -Overfilling if the gauge reads falsely low -Underfilling if the gauge reads high	Gauge not calibrated or calibrated incorrectly	010	Random inspection of gauge calibration	007	350	-100% inspection of incoming gauges -Work with supplier to improve quality -Install overflow value	Shane 4/1	Changed to a more reliable supplier	008	004	002	64
	-Gauge malfunctions -Injury to user from cut glass	Weak or untempered glass	008	Glass breakage test in incoming inspection	008	96	None			008	003	004	96
Broken crystal		Sharp blow to the crystal	009	None		412	Use plastic, break-resistant crystals	Shane 4/1	Tested plastic crystals; now specced into the product	003	003	005	45
Valve Mechanism	Safety pin missing: -Extinguisher engages on its own -Slow leakage empties the tank	Pin falls out because it's too small	010	Incoming inspection on pin diameter	007	140	None			010	007	002	141
		Pin not inserted during manufacturing	009	None		810	Issue the pin supply in exact quantities; in exact quantities for the number of extinguishers	Tyler 3/15	Changed mfg. system to issue all required assembly materials in exact quantities	010	003	003	90
	Handle freezes: User will be unable to discharge the extinguisher	Handle becomes rusted	010	Rust-inhibiting metal used	005	450	Switch to a rust-preventing metal	Kevin 4/1	Supplier is now using zinc plating	010	003	003	90
		Spring in handle too tight	001	Incoming inspection on springs	004	40	None			010	004	001	40

Total RPN Before Action: 4,322

Total RPN After Action: 1,633

When and Where to Use FMEAs

The FMEA process is widely applicable in a variety of settings beyond the product design and manufacturing processes focused on in this book. FMEAs provide a structure and a common language that can be used by teams in manufacturing and service, profit and not-for-profit, private, public, or governmental organizations. FMEA is not just a tool for the manufacturing or engineering department. It can be used to improve support processes, not just manufacturing processes or product design. A discussion of some of the support processes where FMEA might be useful follows.

Safety

FMEAs were first developed as a tool to identify and correct safety hazards. The FMEA process was developed to anticipate and eliminate safety problems before they occurred. Consequently, they can be used to improve the safety of the process of manufacturing a product as well as to improve the safety performance of the product itself.

Manufacturing safety FMEAs should be conducted by a team of people who operate the equipment along with others who are not involved in operating the equipment. This combination of user knowledge and outsider observations provides a comprehensive analysis of the hazards.

FMEAs conducted on products to determine their safety are critical in todays litigious society. Companies have an obligation to assure their customers that their products are safe and fit for use. In many cases, it is not sufficient that product instructions spell out safe operating procedures; safety provisions must be built into the products. It is helpful to involve consumers or eventual users of the product in such an FMEA. They should be asked to use the product, and other members of the FMEA team should observe how it is used. It is not unusual for a product to be incorrectly used or to be used for an unintended purpose. If these possibilities can be uncovered during an FMEA, safeguards can be built into the product design.

Accounting/Finance

With some modifications to the rating scales for severity, occurrence, and detection, FMEAs can be helpful in determining financial strategies and assessing credit or investment risks. For example, before extending substantial credit to a potential customer with a shaky credit history, an FMEA that studies the things that could go wrong with customer credit and how credit failures would affect the company would provide a structure for a credit plan that will reduce financial risk.

Software Design

The effects of software are all around us. Practically everything that we do is governed by software. Software quality assurance is critical in many of these instances. For example, computer systems and the software that drives them are used in air transportation, medicine, and banking, to name a few applications. Problems created by software bugs or incorrect programs can range from nuisances to potentially fatal disasters. As with a product or design FMEA, a software design quality FMEA can identify problems before they occur, so they can be eliminated or reduced.

Information Systems/Technology

Even without software problems, computer glitches can happen because of hardware or systems issues. From the simplest local area network (LAN) to multi-million-dollar telecommunications systems, use of FMEAs can help make both the design and installation of information systems more robust.

Marketing

Billions of dollars are spent on marketing and advertising by U.S. firms annually. Some promotional campaigns are wildly successful, while others are financial busts. An FMEA conducted prior to an advertising or marketing launch can help businesses avoid costly and sometimes embarrassing mistakes. An FMEA can be used to identify offensive or misleading advertising copy. It can also be used to preplan reaction and response to potentially damaging product recalls or disasters.

Human Resources

With organizational restructuring (downsizing, rightsizing), the human resources field is faced with developing and executing plans for new organizational structures that are significantly different from the classic pyramid structures we are all familiar with. Changes on paper that appear to be workable can turn into disaster in reality. An FMEA can be used as a bridge between the plan and the actual restructuring. It forces a structured analysis of problems and glitches that must happen. Plans can be designed to address the potential problems, and crises can be avoided, saving time and money while improving morale.

Purchasing

Prior to purchasing a major piece of equipment, an FMEA can be conducted to anticipate problems with different purchase options. This information can be used to improve purchasing decisions as well as to develop installation plans once the equipment is purchased.

Table 6 provides specific examples of how FMEAs have been used outside of the design and manufacturing areas.

Table 6. Other Uses for FMEAs

Function	Examples
Safety	A plastics molder conducted an FMEA on a new piece of molding equipment to ensure that its safety devices on it worked and that emergency stop buttons were properly placed.
Accounting/Finance	A finance department performed an FMEA on its annual budget to make sure it was realistic and accounted for potential emergency expenses.
Software Design	A firm that develops CAD software used an FMEA to uncover bugs in the system prior to release for beta testing.
Information Systems/Technology	The information systems department conducted an FMEA to determine the security of sensitive data.
Marketing	During the development of a new corporate brochure, the marketing department incorporated an FMEA into the design process to reduce the potential of offending potential customers and miscommunicating vital information about the company.
Human Resources	An HR department led an FMEA that involved senior managers from all departments during an organizational restructuring.
Purchasing	Working with the process engineering department, a purchasing group used an FMEA to select a new piece of manufacturing equipment.

Appendix 1: Creating a Process Flowchart

Flowcharts are to manufacturing processes as road maps are to drivers. They provide a detailed view of the process, and increase understanding of how the process flows. With a process flowchart, teams can identify repetitive steps, bottlenecks, and inefficiencies in the process. When used with an FMEA, they increase the team's understanding of the process, which in turn helps the team identify potential failures, effects, and solutions.

The best way to create a flowchart is to walk through the process as if you were the thing being processed or created. The process steps should be followed sequentially, and notes should be taken during the walk-through.

Once the walk-through is complete, each step should be listed on a self-stick note. It helps to have several people do this, as each will contribute ideas that others missed. The steps should then be grouped and organized according to their order in the process.

For complicated processes with several steps and substeps, it helps to create a top-down flowchart, where each of the major steps in the process are listed in order of flow across the top of the chart and the sub-steps are listed underneath each major step (see Figures 7 and 8).

Once the steps are identified and put in order, sym-

Figure 7. Flow Chart Symbols

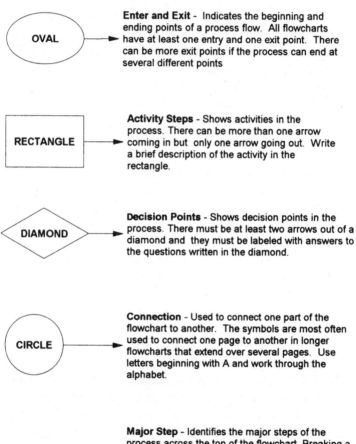

Enter and Exit - Indicates the beginning and ending points of a process flow. All flowcharts have at least one entry and one exit point. There can be more exit points if the process can end at several different points

Activity Steps - Shows activities in the process. There can be more than one arrow coming in but only one arrow going out. Write a brief description of the activity in the rectangle.

Decision Points - Shows decision points in the process. There must be at least two arrows out of a diamond and they must be labeled with answers to the questions written in the diamond.

Connection - Used to connect one part of the flowchart to another. The symbols are most often used to connect one page to another in longer flowcharts that extend over several pages. Use letters beginning with A and work through the alphabet.

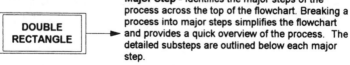

Major Step - Identifies the major steps of the process across the top of the flowchart. Breaking a process into major steps simplifies the flowchart and provides a quick overview of the process. The detailed substeps are outlined below each major step.

Figure 8. Top-Down Flowchart

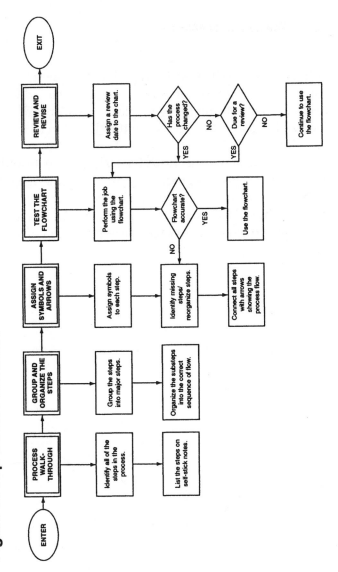

61

bols are assigned to each step. At this point, missed steps become more obvious and can be added as needed. With all the steps in place, arrows connecting the symbols are added to show the direction of the process flow.

As a final step, the flowchart should be tested by walking through the process again, this time using the chart as a guide. Corrections should be made, and a process should be established to review and revise the flowchart periodically to make sure it is kept current.

Appendix 2: Brainstorming

Brainstorming is a well-known technique for generating a large number of ideas in a short period of time. There are many different ways to brainstorm, depending on the objectives of the session. A round-robin approach works best for FMEAs, because it allows each person the opportunity to express their ideas, while keeping the creativity level high.

The round-robin approach to brainstorming allows each person to contribute one idea each time it is his or her turn. Participants should come to the brainstorming meeting with a list of ideas to contribute to the process. New ideas are generated as participants ''piggyback,'' or are inspired by and build on, others' ideas. To encourage creative ideas, no idea should be critiqued or commented on when offered. Each idea should be listed and numbered, exactly as offered, on a flipchart. Expect to generate at least 50 to 60 ideas in a 30-minute brainstorming session.

It helps to review the rules of round-robin-style brainstorming with the group before the session begins.

Brainstorming Rules

1. Do not comment on, judge, or critique ideas as offered.
2. Encourage creative and offbeat ideas.
3. A large number of ideas is the goal.
4. Evaluate ideas later.

When the brainstorming session is over, the ideas should be reviewed, similar ideas combined, and ideas that seem not to fit eliminated.

Appendix 3: Reaching Consensus on Severity, Occurrence, and Detection Ratings

Consensus means that all team members can support the team decision. Ideally, everyone on the FMEA team would agree on the severity, occurrence, and detection ratings. In all likelihood, however, there will be some disagreements, due to each team member's unique perspective of the process or product. Disagreements without a structured process to address and resolve them can waste a lot of time and energy. The team should agree, in advance, on a process to handle disagreements. Outlined below are some methods to help reach consensus.

Team Voting

Voting and ranking is a vehicle to help the team reach consensus on severity, occurrence, and detection ratings. When there is disagreement on a rating, team members who feel strongly about their ratings should present their rationale for the rating to the rest of the team. If necessary, a time limit (for example, five minutes each) can be put on these presentations. Linking their argument to the predefined rating scale will help strengthen their position. When the presentations are complete, team members should cast their votes for what they feel the rating should be. The mean (arithmetic average) rating should be calculated and used as a reference point for the team to arrive at a consensus score.

It is important not to take the mean score as the "score" without any additional discussion. The voting process is a consensus reaching tool, but it alone cannot ensure that the entire team supports the rating.

If the voting process does not help the group arrive at consensus, there are a few other exercises the team can work through to reach agreement.

Get the Process Expert Involved

If the process expert is not on your team, you might want to invite him or her to a meeting to review the FMEA ratings and give an opinion about how the item in question should be rated. The expert should not have the final say in the rating, but rather should provide the team with information that perhaps they didn't know or weren't aware of. The team has the final say.

Defer to One of the Team Members

Your team could assign one member of the team to make the final decision if there is a person on the team with a lot of expertise on the product or process. The problem with this approach is that there is a chance some team members might not agree with the rating and, in turn, will have a difficult time supporting the FMEA from this point on.

Rank Failures and/or Effects Within a Rating Category

List each failure and effect on a self-stick note. Do not worry about the actual score of the rating in question. Instead, put the failures in order (from the highest to the lowest) according to the scale in question. For example, if the scale in question is severity and the team is unable to reach agreement on the rating of two or more of the failure modes, put each of the failure modes on a self-stick note. Then, as a team, put the failure modes in order from the highest severity to the lowest severity. At this point, you should not be concerned with the numerical rating for the failure modes. Once the failures are in order, indicate the ratings for any of the failure modes that the team has been able to agree upon. By thinking of the failures relative to each other, rather than in terms of an absolute scale, you may be able to agree on the ratings for the failure modes in dispute.

Talking It Out

Because the ratings are multiplied, a one- or two-point difference on any one of the rating scales can have a significant impact on the RPN for the failure mode. The difference could put the item below the cut-off point, when it should be above the cut-off. This would mean that a relatively high-risk failure would not be eliminated or reduced. Therefore, it is risky to assign ratings arbitrarily just to move along in the FMEA process. Sometimes the best way to reach consensus on a particularly sticky issue is to talk it out.

Use the Higher Rating

If the team just can't reach consensus, the team might elect to use the higher rating. The only thing lost here is the time it takes to work on another item. There could be tremendous gains to using this approach and operating on the safe side.

Appendix 4: Process Improvement Techniques

Organizations have a wide variety of approaches to improvement available to them once an improvement opportunity has been identified. The improvement opportunities identified through an FMEA are no exception. Some effective techniques for following through on identified opportunities are described briefly below.

Mistake-Proofing

Mistake-proofing techniques, when implemented properly, make it impossible to have a failure. An excellent example of mistake-proofing is a car that won't start unless the clutch pedal is depressed. This prevents the car from lurching forward when it is started. Before this was mistake-proofed, a driver could try to start the car while it was in gear, causing it to jump forward into other cars, objects, and even people.

Mistake-proofing techniques include ways to make it impossible to make mistakes in both the manufacture and use of products. Limit switches, electric eyes, bar coding, and counting techniques can all be used to mistake-proof processes and products.

Examples of mistake-proofing we experience every day include the following:

- Electric heaters that turn off if they fall over.

- Car lights that shut off automatically.

- Overwrite protection tabs on audio and video tapes and computer disks.

- Irons that shut off after being unused for a set number of minutes.

- Automatic seat belts.

Design of Experiments

Design of experiments or DOE is a family of statistical techniques that first help identify the key variables in a process, and then determine the optimum processing parameters for the highest quality. Design of experiments is effective in both continuous and discrete processes. DOE can be used in the product development stage as well.

There are many types of DOEs. Full factorials, fractional factorials, response surface methodology, and EVOP (evolutionary operations) are some. Perhaps the most powerful type of DOE is the family of extreme fractional factorial designs called screening experiments.

Using a screening experiment, it is possible to vary several process variables at the same time and statistically determine which variables or combination of variables have the greatest impact on the process outcomes. Once these key variables are known, the FMEA team can focus its efforts just on these variables, saving time, effort, and money.

Statistical Process Control

Statistical Process Control, or SPC, another statistical technique, is a tool that can be used to monitor processes to make sure they haven't changed or to compare the output of a process to specification. One SPC technique, control charting, enables operators to monitor key process variables and adjust the process when it changes, before it goes out of control and produces bad product.

The FMEA team can use control charts to get a real-time view of the process. When a failure occurs in the process, the control charts will signal a change. By quickly reacting to the signal, the team can work to find the root cause of the failure before the trail gets cold. Once the root cause is found, mistake-proofing can be used to eliminate the failure mode, taking the resulting RPN to zero.

Team Problem-Solving Using CI Tools

Many processes and products can be improved using basic continuous improvement tools and the brain-power of the improvement team. Basic well-known improvement tools include brainstorming, flowcharting, data collection and analysis, voting and ranking, Pareto analysis, cause and effect analysis, and action planning.

Appendix 5: QS-9000 Requirements for FMEAs

QS-9000 is the Quality Systems Requirement originally developed by the Chrysler/Ford/General Motors Supplier Quality Requirements Task Force. Their goal was to develop a fundamental quality system that provides for continuous improvement, emphasizing defect prevention and the reduction of waste in the supply chain.

The basis of QS-9000 is ISO 9000 with heavy emphasis on ISO 9001, Section 4. It is supplemented with additional interpretations and quality system requirements and applies to all internal and external suppliers of production materials, production or service parts, heat treating, painting, plating, or other finishing services directly to Chrysler, Ford, General Motors, and manufacturers subscribing to the standard.

While the ISO 9000 standard specifies what companies must do in terms of their quality systems, QS-9000 goes into more detail on how companies should operationalize the standard.

Quality System Element 4.2 states that:

The supplier shall define and document how the requirements for quality will be met. Quality planning shall be consistent with all other requirements of a supplier's quality system and shall be documented in a format to suit the supplier's method of operation. The supplier shall give consideration to the following activities, as appropriate, in meeting the specified requirements for products, projects or contracts. . .

Element 4.2.3.c specifically identifies:

Ensuring the compatibility of the design, the production process, installation, servicing, inspection, and test procedures and the applicable documentation.

QS-9000 goes on to specify:

Suppliers shall establish and implement an advanced product quality planning process. Suppliers should convene internal cross-functional teams to prepare for production of new or changed products . . .

It states that among other things team actions should include:

- *Development and review of FMEAs.*

- *Establishment of actions to reduce the potential failure modes with high risk priority numbers.*

In describing the role of FMEAs, the QS-9000 standard states:

Process FMEAs shall consider all special characteristics. Efforts shall be taken to improve the process to achieve defect prevention rather than defect detection. Certain customers have FMEA review and approval requirements that shall be met prior to production part approval.

FMEA GLOSSARY OF TERMS

Design of experiments (DOE)   A series of statistical techniques used to introduce controlled change into a process and to study the effect of the change on the process outcomes.

Detection   The FMEA rating scale that defines the likelihood of detecting a failure or the effect of the failure before it occurs.

FMEA   The acronym for Failure Mode and Effect Analysis, a systematic, structured approach to process improvement in the design and process development stage.

ISO 9000   International quality standards for product design, manufacture, and distribution.

Mistake-proofing   Making the process so robust that it cannot fail.

Occurrence   The FMEA rating scale that defines the frequency of a failure mode.

QS-9000   Automotive sector-specific quality requirements.

Resulting RPN   The risk priority number of a failure mode and its corresponding effect(s) after improvement.

Risk Priority Number (RPN)   The risk priority number of a failure mode and its effect(s) before improvement.

Severity   The FMEA rating scale that defines the seriousness and severity of the effect of the failure, should it occur.

Statistical process control (SPC)   A statistical technique used to monitor processes, usually involving the use of control charts.

Total RPN   The sum of all RPNs in a given FMEA.